AN ADVENT OF MIRACLES

A MOTHER-DAUGHTER JOURNEY THROUGH TWENTY-FIVE DAYS OF LOVE AND LIGHT

LAURA DOVER

Paperback ISBN: 978-1-959993-64-3
Ebook ISBN: 978-1-959993-65-0
Hardback ISBN: 978-1-959993-66-7
Audio ISBN: 978-1-959993-67-4

Net worlding
PUBLISHING

I dedicate this book to my daughter Mary, my little ray of light.

A Treasure to keep for Mother and Daughter. This journal can be used during the 25 days leading up to Christmas to rediscover your bond. It serves as a gentle reminder of the importance of the relationship between a Mom and a Daughter, not only over the season, but over a lifetime.

CONTENTS

DAY 1 – THE COUNTDOWN BEGINS

The first snow arrived like a sigh, gentle, quiet, and just enough to soften the sharp edges of the world.

Emma Bennett stood at the kitchen counter; hands wrapped around a mug of coffee that had long since gone lukewarm. She stared out the window at the flakes drifting past the porch light and smiled faintly. She'd always loved this part — the quiet before December woke up, when the air seemed to hold its breath, and hope hadn't yet grown complicated.

From the living room came the faint hum of a phone and a teenage sigh that could only belong to her daughter.

Elizabeth Bennett, fourteen and full of contradictions — all rolled eyes and earbuds one minute, all wonder and warmth the next — was sprawled on the couch, scrolling through her phone, pretending not to listen to her mother hum "Have Yourself a Merry Little Christmas." Her Mother and friends called her Lizzy for short because they claimed she was "full of energy and life".

Emma took a breath, straightened the small table by the window, and reached for the worn wooden box sitting on the shelf. Its paint was chipped and faded, the once-bright red now a muted cranberry, the gold numbers dulled by time.

Still, when the light hit it just right, it seemed to shimmer faintly, as if remembering all the Decembers it had survived.

She ran a thumb over the carved lid. "Well, old friend," she murmured, "let's see what you have for us this year."

Lizzy groaned from the couch. "Please don't tell me that's what I think it is."

Emma smiled, carrying it carefully to the coffee table. "It's the advent calendar, yes."

Lizzy looked up, one eyebrow raised. "The haunted advent calendar."

Emma laughed. "It's not haunted, it's historic. Your grandmother made it with your great-grandfather when she was about your age."

Lizzy smirked. "So... haunted."

Emma sat beside her, brushing a strand of hair from

her face. "It's tradition, sweetheart. Every day, we open a door and find something that reminds us of what Christmas is really about."

Lizzy shrugged, half teasing, half softening. "Can't we just download an app for that?"

Emma chuckled. "Where's the fun in that?"

She lifted the lid and revealed the tiny wooden doors; each painted with a number from 1 to 25. Time had worn their edges smooth, and one hinge creaked faintly, like an old story stretching awake.

Lizzy leaned in despite herself. "So, what happens if we open one?"

Emma's smile turned wistful. "Then, my love, the countdown begins. Twenty-five days to remember who we are... and maybe to become someone new."

Lizzy tilted her head. "That sounds suspiciously like one of your 'life lesson' speeches."

Emma grinned. "It's a mother's duty to sprinkle those in where she can."

She brushed her fingers over the first little door and opened it. Inside was a tiny slip of paper, yellowed around the edges. Her mother's handwriting curved across it in faded ink:

Day One: have gratitude, even when you don't yet understand what you've been given.

Lizzy read it over her shoulder, her voice quiet. "Grandma wrote that?"

Emma nodded, smiling softly. "Every year, she'd tuck something inside. Little reminders. I used to think she was just being sentimental."

Lizzy studied her mother for a moment — the way she traced the letters with her finger, the way her eyes softened when she said the word "Grandma."

Emma placed the note back in the calendar and closed the door gently. "It's funny," she said, almost to herself. "Every year, I tell myself it's just a tradition. But somehow, by the time we reach the twenty-fifth, it always feels like something's changed. Like we've both changed."

Lizzy smiled faintly. "Even me?"

Emma looked at her and smiled — not the patient, parental kind of smile, but the knowing one. "Especially you."

Lizzy laughed softly. "You're really leaning into the Christmas magic thing, huh?"

Emma's eyes twinkled. "Maybe I just believe that small things have the power to turn into miracles if we give them time."

Lizzy looked back at the calendar, tracing the gold-painted number 1. For a moment, she thought she saw the tiniest glint of light shimmer beneath it — but when she blinked, it was gone.

She frowned, then smiled. "Okay, Mom. Let's see what your old box can do."

Emma laughed, pressing her hand over Lizzy's. "You might be surprised."

Outside, the wind picked up, scattering flakes across the windowpane. Inside, mother and daughter sat side by side — not realizing that the twenty-five little doors waiting ahead would open more than memories.

They would open each other.

Reflection: Some traditions are more than a memory; they were an invitation to something greater. Every December, we are offered 25 chances to rediscover what it means to love, to hope, and to believe again.

Mother's Note: What traditions do you hope your daughter will remember most? How do you feel at the start of the season?

_____

_____

_____

_____

Daughter's Note: What is the one thing you love (or secretly like) about the holidays? What do you hope this month will bring?

_____

_____

_____

_____

DAY 2 – THE ORNAMENT BOX

The Saturday sunlight spilled across the floor as Lizzy knelt beside a big cardboard box marked Christmas Decorations. The handwriting, slanted and familiar, belonged to her mom, written years ago in red marker.

"Do we really have to use all the same stuff?" Lizzy asked, tugging at the tape. "We could just... I don't know, start over this year. Something new."

Emma smiled as she sat down beside her. "We could. But half the fun is remembering what's already in here."

Lizzy sighed playfully. "You and your memories."

Emma winked. "Guilty as charged."

EMMA PULLED open the box flap, releasing a little puff of dust and the faint scent of pine. Inside were layers of ornaments—shiny, handmade, and a few clearly loved past their prime. She reached for the first ornament in the box—tiny clay angel wings painted in glitter. "You made this one in second grade. The glitter was still on my hands at Easter."

Lizzy set her phone down. "I remember that craft day. I got in trouble for putting glue in my hair."

"I remember washing it out," Emma said warmly. "Twice."

They laughed together, the sound light and familiar. For the first time this December, the air between them felt easy again.

Lizzy then reached in and picked up a small glass ornament, round and delicate with gold swirls across its surface.

"Wow," Lizzy said. "This one's pretty—"

But before she could finish, the ornament slipped between her fingers and landed softly on the hardwood floor with a crack.

Both of them froze.

"Oh," Emma said quietly, blinking. For a heartbeat, disappointment flickered across her face—gone almost as soon as it appeared. "It's alright," she added quickly, her tone bright again. "It's just a little break. We've still got plenty of others."

Lizzy crouched down, picking up a few small shards. "Was this one special?"

Emma smiled, though it didn't quite reach her eyes. "Your grandma gave it to me when I was your age. It's been through a lot of Christmases."

Lizzy looked at the fragments glinting in her palm, then up at her mother. "I'm sorry, Mom."

"It's okay, sweetheart," Emma said gently, brushing the dust from her hands. "Honestly, I'm amazed it lasted this long." She forced a light laugh and reached into the box again. "Now—let's find one that's not breakable, shall we?"

Lizzy smiled back, but as her mom turned away, she studied the broken ornament on the floor for a moment longer. It caught a bit of sunlight and sparkled—still beautiful, even in pieces.

She didn't say anything, but an idea began to form in the back of her mind.

Reflection: Even the most fragile things can shine again with a little care and imagination.

Mother's Note: Think of something in your life that felt broken but taught you strength. What do you see when you look in your daughter's eyes during the season?

_____

_____

_____

_____

Daughter's Note: What does it feel like when you make a mistake? Are you able to forgive your own actions? How does it feel when your mom reacts in a way you were not expecting?

_____

_____

_____

_____

DAY 3 – HOT COCOA NIGHT

By the time the snow started to fall, Lizzy had already claimed her favorite spot on the couch—wrapped in a blanket, scrolling on her phone.

From the kitchen, Emma's voice floated through the air. "It's snowing!"

Lizzy barely glanced up. "Cool."

Emma peeked around the corner, one eyebrow raised. "That's all you've got. 'Cool?' You used to run to the window like it was magic."

Lizzy smirked. "I was seven. Everything was magic when I was seven."

"Well," Emma said, turning back toward the kitchen, "some of us still believe in magic. Especially the kind that comes in a mug."

Lizzy's head popped up. "Wait—are you making cocoa?"

"Maybe," Emma teased. "But it's for people who appreciate snowfall."

That was all it took. A moment later, Lizzy was in the kitchen, blanket still draped around her shoulders like a cape. "Okay, fine," she said, leaning on the counter. "I'm officially appreciating it. Snow, cocoa, magic—whatever."

Emma smiled, whisking the cocoa until it frothed. The smell of chocolate and cinnamon filled the room, rich and comforting. She slid one mug toward her daughter. "No marshmallows?"

Lizzy gasped dramatically. "What kind of operation are you running here?" She opened a cupboard, found the bag, and dumped in at least a dozen.

Emma laughed. "That's not cocoa anymore—that's a dessert buffet."

Emma handed her a mug and nodded toward the whipped cream. "You do the honors."

Lizzy grinned, taking a sip. "Perfect."

For a few minutes, they stood together at the window, sipping in silence as the snow drifted past the porch light. The world outside looked soft, almost dreamlike.

"You know," Lizzy said, her voice quieter now, "this isn't terrible."

Emma smiled without looking away from the window. "I'll take that as a compliment."

Lizzy bumped her shoulder lightly against her mom's. "It's a pretty low bar, but yeah—you should."

They both laughed, the kind of laughter that comes easily once the tension finally melts away.

Reflection: Sometimes the smallest moments—like cocoa and snow—remind us that joy doesn't have to shout to be heard.

Mother's Note: Describe a moment you felt close to your daughter either during the season or another point in time. What emotions does it evoke?

_____

_____

_____

_____

Daughter's Note: Are there instances that you would like to be closer to your mom, but struggle. Describe that in more detail.

_____

_____

_____

_____

DAY 4 – THE MUSIC OF DECEMBER

The morning started with music. Not just any music, Emma's favorite Christmas playlist, the one she'd been playing every December since Lizzy could walk.

The first notes of Silver Bells floated through the house like cinnamon in the air—sweet, familiar, and, to Lizzy, just a little too loud for 9 a.m.

From her bedroom, she shouted, "Mom! Are you seriously doing this already?"

Emma's voice came from the kitchen. "Doing what?"

"Blasting Christmas carols before I've even had breakfast!"

"That's what December's for!" Emma called back, cheerful and unapologetic.

Lizzy groaned dramatically, pulling her blanket over

her head, but she couldn't completely tune out the melody. She'd grown up with those songs. They were the soundtrack to cookie baking, snow forts, and wrapping paper chaos. Still—she'd never admit that to her mom.

When she finally wandered into the kitchen, the air smelled like toast and cocoa from the night before. Emma hummed along with the song as she flipped pancakes, using the spatula like a microphone.

Lizzy rolled her eyes. "You're embarrassing yourself."

Emma grinned. "Maybe, but I'm having fun doing it." She sang the next line, deliberately off-key.

Lizzy smirked despite herself. "You know the neighbors can probably hear you."

"Good," Emma said with a wink. "Maybe they'll join in."

Lizzy sat at the table, pretending to scroll on her phone, but when "Frosty the Snowman" started, she caught herself mouthing the words.

Emma noticed but said nothing.

By the time breakfast was done, Lizzy was tapping her foot under the table. She didn't realize it until Emma started laughing softly.

"What?" Lizzy asked.

"Nothing," Emma said, pouring another cup of coffee. "Just enjoying the music."

Lizzy shook her head, trying to hide her smile. "You're so weird."

Emma raised her mug. "And you're secretly singing along."

Lizzy laughed, and for a moment, the house felt just like it used to—warm, loud, and a little off-key, but perfectly them.

Reflection: Sometimes the songs we resist the most are the ones our hearts already know by heart.

Mother's Note: Describe how music can often heal your soul? What are the songs that offer you healing in difficult times?

_____

_____

_____

_____

Daughter's Note: How does music make you feel? Does it ever transform your mood over the holidays or other times when you are feeling down?

_____

_____

_____

_____

DAY 5 – THE SNOWFLAKE MOMENT

The snow had been falling all morning, thick, lazy flakes that drifted down in no hurry at all. By the time the world outside turned white, Emma stood at the window, mug in hand, smiling to herself.

"Mom," Lizzy groaned from the couch, "you're doing it again."

"Doing what?"

"Staring out the window like it's a movie."

Emma turned, her eyes soft with amusement. "It is a movie. A classic called First Snow of December. I've seen it every year, and somehow it never gets old."

Lizzy smirked. "Pretty sure it's got the same plot every time."

"Maybe," Emma said, setting her mug down, "but the ending's always different, depending on who decides to go outside."

Lizzy raised an eyebrow. "Oh no. I know where this is going."

"Come on," Emma coaxed, already pulling on her coat. "You can't scroll through snow, Lizzy."

Lizzy laughed, half protesting as her mom handed her a hat. "Ugh, fine. But if I lose a toe, I'm blaming you."

Minutes later, they stepped into the yard, their boots crunching through fresh powder. The air was sharp and bright, each breath puffing out like tiny clouds.

Emma tilted her head back, catching a snowflake on her glove. "You used to think each one had a personality," she said. "You'd name them—Snowy, Fluffy, Sparkle..."

Lizzy grinned in spite of herself. "Wow, I was adorable."

"You were," Emma agreed. "Still are."

Lizzy rolled her eyes but smiled. "You're biased."

"Completely."

They walked through the yard, the world muffled and soft. Emma inhaled deeply, letting the cold sting her cheeks—it reminded her of winters when Lizzy was small, bundled in bright mittens, giggling as she rolled snowballs bigger than herself.

"Should we build one?" Emma asked suddenly.

Lizzy crossed her arms. "A snowman? Really?"

Emma nodded toward the untouched patch of snow. "Unless you're afraid I'll outbuild you."

"Oh, it's on," Lizzy said, dropping to her knees with mock determination.

For the next twenty minutes, the yard filled with laughter and shouts of "that's too lopsided!" and "your snowball's cheating!" Their snowman leaned slightly, his head a little off-center, but when Emma stepped back, brushing snow from her gloves, she couldn't stop smiling.

"He's perfect," she said.

Lizzy snorted. "He's definitely something."

Emma looped her arm around her daughter's shoulders. "We used to call that kind of perfect."

Lizzy looked at the snowman again—his crooked grin, the scarf that didn't match—and quietly said, "Yeah... maybe it still is."

For a long moment, neither of them spoke. The snow kept falling, covering their boots, softening the world around them.

Emma's heart swelled, full of memory and something new; joy not from the past, but from the moment right here, snow melting on her lashes and her daughter laughing beside her.

REFLECTION: Sometimes the best memories aren't the ones we remember, they're the ones we make all over again.

Mother's Note: What childlike joy did you still experience? Does your daughter remind you of your younger self in any way?

_____

_____

_____

_____

Daughter's Note: If you could create "the perfect day", what would it look like? Does it surprise you when your inner child comes back to visit?

_____

_____

_____

_____

DAY 6 – BAKING DAY

By mid-morning, the kitchen was already alive with the sound of mixing bowls and holiday music. Emma tied her old red apron around her waist — the one splattered with years of memories — and smiled as she set out ingredients.

Lizzy wandered in, still in her pajamas, hair pulled into a messy bun. "Let me guess," she said, spotting the flour and sugar. "It's cookie day?"

"Of course," Emma said cheerfully. "It's tradition."

Lizzy smirked, grabbing a mixing spoon. "Then let me handle it. I've got this."

Emma blinked, amused. "Oh really? You're suddenly head baker?"

Lizzy shrugged with teenage confidence. "I've seen enough baking shows. How hard can it be?"

Emma stepped back, watching as Lizzy measured

flour — sort of — and cracked eggs with more enthusiasm than accuracy. The kitchen quickly filled with the scent of vanilla and the soft rhythm of music playing from Lizzy's phone.

"Careful with that mixer—" Emma started, but Lizzy waved her off. "Mom, I got it!"

The mixer sputtered, coughed, and sent a small puff of flour into the air. Both froze, then burst out laughing.

Emma grabbed a towel, still smiling, though something small and wistful tugged at her chest. She doesn't need me for everything anymore, she thought. And that's exactly how it's supposed to be.

Lizzy looked up, flour dusting her cheeks like snow. "You okay, Mom?"

Emma smiled. "I'm perfect. Keep going, Chef."

When the cookies came out of the oven — slightly uneven but golden — Lizzy announced proudly, "See? I told you. Nailed it."

Emma grinned. "They smell amazing."

Lizzy slid the tray onto the counter and reached for the icing tubes. "Teamwork time?" she asked, offering her mom one.

Emma's heart warmed. "Teamwork," she agreed.

They iced the cookies side by side — one neat and careful, one wildly colorful — their elbows bumping, laughter spilling out between them.

"This one looks like it survived a snowstorm," Emma teased.

Lizzy held it up proudly. "It has character."

Emma laughed, shaking her head. "That's one word for it."

For a moment, the kitchen grew quiet except for the soft hum of the oven and the clink of spoons.

Lizzy broke the silence. "You know," she said, her tone softer now, "I think you're right about traditions. They're kind of... nice."

Emma's eyes softened. "They really are."

Lizzy smiled at her mother, and in that look was something unspoken — gratitude, love, and the faintest echo of the little girl who used to sneak raw cookie dough when she thought no one was watching.

Reflection: Sometimes letting go just means stepping back far enough to see how beautifully they've grown.es

Mother: What is it like to see your daughter grow up? What emotions does it bring to mind?

_____

_____

_____

_____

Daughter: What does it mean to take on more responsibility? Is this something you enjoy? Explain your feelings.

_____

_____

_____

_____

DAY 7 – LETTERS TO SANTA

 hen Emma pulled out the red stationery box from the drawer in the hallway, Lizzy groaned before she even saw it.

"Oh no," she said dramatically. "That's the Santa letter box, isn't it?"

Emma smiled, setting it gently on the table. "It sure is. December seventh. We're right on schedule."

LIZZY FLOPPED INTO A CHAIR. "Mom, you do realize Santa's probably got an email address by now, right?"

Emma chuckled. "He's old-fashioned. Likes the charm of paper. Besides, it's more fun this way."

Lizzy crossed her arms, trying to sound unimpressed.

"I'm just saying — with all the kids in the world, his postage bill must be insane."

Emma laughed, handing her a crisp piece of red paper anyway. "And yet, every year, the magic works out just fine."

Lizzy rolled her eyes but took the paper. "Fine. But only because my handwriting is basically art."

They sat together at the table, the smell of cinnamon drifting from the kitchen, the house warm and soft with light. Emma began writing immediately, her pen looping carefully across the page. Lizzy, on the other hand, just stared at hers for a long moment, pretending she didn't have anything to say.

Finally, she sighed and started writing, mumbling to herself. "Okay, fine. Maybe a few small requests..."

Emma looked up. "Don't forget to add something for someone else. Santa always notices when you do."

Lizzy raised an eyebrow. "You say that like you know him personally."

Emma smiled, that familiar twinkle in her eyes. "Let's just say he and I have excellent correspondence."

Lizzy grinned. "You're so suspiciously confident about this."

"That's called experience," Emma said, sealing her letter with a sticker shaped like a snowflake.

Emma's note read

"*Dear Santa, I wish for happiness for my family and my*

daughter. I wish most of all for this year to be special between us both.

All my Love Emma".

When Lizzy finished hers, she held it up, tapping the corner thoughtfully. Lizzy's read,

Dear Santa, I would like, in no particular order:

1.rotating curling iron

2.new brown boots

3. new comforter for my room

4. a good Christmas for kids that don't have all the things they need

Love Lizzy

Lizzy thought about the list for a moment, wondering if she should ask for her and her mom to have the best Christmas ever, but reluctantly stopped, not wanting to ask the big man for too many requests.

Handing the letter to her mom, Lizzy asked, "So, um... where do these actually go again?"

Emma's smile deepened. "Oh, don't worry. They always get where they need to go. The North Pole has a way of finding letters meant for it."

Lizzy hesitated, then nodded slowly. "Yeah. Guess that makes sense. Magic has good GPS."

Emma laughed softly. "Exactly." They placed their letters side by side on the mantel, just beneath the garland. The glow from the tree lights shimmered against the envelopes, and for a brief, quiet moment, the room seemed to hum — not loudly, but like a secret that only the season itself could hear.

Lizzy didn't say anything more, but when she glanced at her letter again, a small smile curved her lips.

REFLECTION: Some magic doesn't need proof — it just needs to be believed in, one wish at a time

Mother: Why is it important for you to keep magic of the spirit alive? Does this "sense of spirit" resonate in other parts of your life?

_____

_____

_____

_____

Daughter: Why it important for you to embrace the season of Christmas?

_____

_____

_____

_____

DAY 8 - GIVING BACK

The Saturday sky was a silvery gray when Emma stood by the front door, scarf already looped and gloves in hand.

"Ready to go?" she called.

From upstairs, Lizzy's voice drifted down. "Go where?"

Emma smiled. "The community coat drive. It's giving-back day."

Lizzy appeared on the stairs, hoodie half-zipped, skeptical expression firmly in place. "You mean standing outside in the cold... collecting coats... for strangers?"

Emma nodded cheerfully. "Exactly."

Lizzy sighed. "You're so weirdly enthusiastic about hypothermia."

"Come on," Emma said, holding out her coat. "It's good for the heart—and for the circulation."

Lizzy smirked. "I'm sure Santa would totally back that up."

By the time they reached the community center, the cold had pinked their cheeks and turned their breath into clouds. Tables were set up with boxes labeled Winter Wear Donations, and the smell of hot cocoa drifted through the air.

Emma began helping sort the coats by size while Lizzy lingered near the car, arms crossed.

"You didn't bring one to donate?" Emma asked gently.

Lizzy shrugged. "I mean... I have that old blue one, but it's still fine. I like it."

Emma smiled knowingly. "That's fair. Keep it if you need it."

They worked quietly for a while—Emma greeting donors with warm smiles, Lizzy pretending not to be freezing but secretly watching everything unfold.

Then a young woman approached, holding her daughter's hand. The little girl's coat was far too thin, sleeves riding up past her wrists.

Emma knelt down to the child's level. "Hi there. That's a brave color to wear in this weather," she said, admiring the bright pink mittens with holes in them.

The girl grinned shyly. "It's my favorite."

The mother smiled, tired but kind. "We're just hoping they have one that fits her a little better."

Emma nodded softly, her heart tightening. Tears built up in her eyes as she remembered winters like that—

times when her own budget barely stretched far enough for bills, having to put on a smile for the kids and make the holidays fun despite not having the funds. Her heart was heavy and hopeful as she said, "We'll find one," then paused again, "we always do."

Lizzy watched the exchange from a few feet away. Her fingers toyed with the zipper of her own jacket, the newer one, the one she loved—but her thoughts drifted to the blue coat hanging in the car.

A few minutes later, she quietly slipped away and returned with it.

"Hey," she said, approaching the table, "I think this one might fit her."

The little girl's eyes widened as Lizzy held it out. "It's soft," she said, running her hands down the sleeves.

"It's lucky too," Lizzy said with a grin. "It kept me warm every snow day for, like, five years."

The girl smiled, and her mom whispered a soft thank-you, eyes glassy. Emma stood nearby, watching the whole exchange with quiet pride and something deeper—a tenderness shaped by her own memories.

When they got back in the car, Lizzy stared out the window as the snow began to fall again. "I guess I can wear my other one," she said casually.

Emma started the engine, her voice gentle. "You did a really good thing, sweetheart."

Lizzy shrugged, a smile tugging at her lips. "Yeah, well... it looked better on her anyway."

Emma reached over and gave her hand a squeeze. "I think it looked perfect."

For a while, neither said anything. The car was quiet except for the hum of the heater and the soft, steady rhythm of falling snow.

REFLECTION: Sometimes the warmth we give away finds its way right back to us.

Mother's Note: When have you experienced a moment of kindness? How does it feel when your daughter shows compassion?

_____

_____

_____

_____

Daughter's Note: How does it feel to help someone in need? How does it feel when someone returns that kindness to you?

_____

_____

_____

_____

DAY 9 - THE TREE DEBATE

By Sunday afternoon, the house was full of boxes again — ornaments, lights, and one tall cardboard cylinder labeled Artificial Tree – Handle with Joy.

Lizzy plopped onto the couch, sipping cocoa. "We already have the tree. Why are we even talking about this?"

Emma, holding her coat and car keys, smiled. "Because the fake one is missing half its branches, and last year we had to tape it to the wall so it wouldn't lean."

Lizzy grinned. "That's called creativity."

Emma shook her head, laughing. "That's called an engineering emergency."

She jingled her keys. "Come on, we're going tree shopping."

Lizzy groaned. "Mom, the real ones shed. And they smell like—like outdoors."

"That's the point," Emma said. "Christmas is supposed to smell like pine and fresh air."

Lizzy countered, "It's supposed to smell like cinnamon candles and cookies. You know, the indoor version of joy."

Emma chuckled. "Okay, tell you what: if we find a tree that passes your indoor test, we'll get it. If not, we'll drag the old one out of the basement again and name it Leany, the Tree Part II."

That got Lizzy moving. "Fine. But only because Leany deserves retirement."

The lot smelled of pine and cold air, lights strung overhead twinkling against the gray sky. Emma wandered between the rows, humming softly, while Lizzy trailed behind, pretending not to be impressed.

"They're so big," Lizzy said, eyeing the rows of evergreens. "We could fit, like, three apartments inside one of these."

Emma laughed. "Or one very happy Christmas."

Lizzy crossed her arms. "Real trees are high maintenance."

"Like someone else I know," Emma teased.

Lizzy gasped, feigning offense. "Rude."

"Accurate."

They both laughed.

Then Emma stopped in front of a medium-sized tree,

not the tallest or fullest, but balanced and soft-looking. She brushed her hand along its branches. "This one feels right," she said quietly.

Lizzy tilted her head. "You say that like it's a person."

Emma smiled. "In this family, trees have personalities. Remember Snowbert?"

"How could I forget? He dropped half his needles on my math homework."

"Character building," Emma said, winking.

Lizzy sighed, looking around once more. "Okay, fine. This one's... nice."

Emma's smile widened. "Nice enough for a cinnamon-candle household?"

Lizzy shrugged. "We'll see."

They loaded it onto the car roof, laughing at their uneven knots, and when they got home, the scent of pine filled the living room. Lizzy pretended to sneeze dramatically but secretly smiled as the room came alive with lights.

Emma stepped back to admire it. "What do you think?"

Lizzy squinted at the slightly crooked star on top. "He's a little lopsided."

Emma nodded. "Perfect, then."

Lizzy grinned. "Yeah. Perfect."

REFLECTION: Sometimes compromise is where the magic hides — a little give, a little laugh, and a tree that leans just right.

Mother's Note: Do you think there is beauty in imperfection? Explain your reasoning behind your answer....

Daughter's Note: What happens when things don't go as planned? Can you think of a time that it didn't....... How did it turn out for you?

DAY 10 – THE ORNAMENT RESTORED

The living room glowed softly with golden light. The tree stood proudly in the corner, branches full but waiting for the final touches. Emma reached up, stretching to hang a small glass angel near the top. It slipped from her fingers once, and she caught it just in time, laughing quietly to herself.

From across the room, Lizzy watched. She noticed how carefully her mom handled each ornament, how her smile was real, but her eyes held that faint, wistful shine that always came with December.

"Need help?" Lizzy asked, trying to sound casual.

Emma glanced down from the step stool. "I think I've got it, but thank you." She smiled, though she looked a little tired.

Lizzy hesitated, then walked to the table where the

last few ornaments waited. "You missed one," she said softly.

Emma turned — and froze.

In Lizzy's hands was the ornament — the one that had broken weeks ago. Only now, it gleamed softly in the light, the cracks traced with a swirl of golden glue and a few tiny flecks of sparkle that caught the glow of the tree.

Emma's breath caught. "Lizzy... you fixed it?"

Lizzy nodded, a little shy. "I wanted to surprise you. I used the gold paint from your craft drawer and... well, it's not perfect, but—"

Emma stepped down from the stool and took the ornament carefully in her hands. "It's perfect," she whispered, her voice trembling slightly.

Lizzy smiled. "I just thought... you said Grandma gave it to you. So maybe one day, I'll pass it on too. Kind of like a mom-to-daughter tradition."

Emma blinked back tears, her heart swelling with pride and love. "That's exactly what she would have wanted."

Lizzy grinned, holding the branch steady while Emma hung it near the center of the tree. The light hit it just right, making it shimmer more beautifully than before.

Emma stepped back, her voice barely above a whisper. "You gave it new life."

Lizzy shrugged, smiling softly. "Guess it was just waiting for its next chapter."

They stood together for a long moment, the room quiet except for the faint sound of carols playing in the background. The tree sparkled with light — but somehow, that single ornament seemed to shine brightest of all.

Reflection: Love is what turns what's fragile into something that lasts — passed from one heart, one generation, one Christmas to the next.

Mother's Note: What does it feel like when someone shows you compassion that you weren't expecting?

_____

_____

_____

_____

Daughter's Note: Was does it feel like to show compassion for others? Do you think you could show this to a person who has been unkind to you in the past?

_____

_____

_____

_____

DAY 11 – CHRISTMAS CARDS

The kitchen table had disappeared under a sea of envelopes, stamps, and sparkly pens. Emma sat surrounded by a gentle mess of holiday stationery, her handwriting looping gracefully across a stack of Christmas cards.

Lizzy entered, holding her phone and a mug of cocoa. "Whoa," she said, eyeing the pile. "Are you writing... actual cards?"

Emma smiled. "Of course. It's Christmas card day."

Lizzy tilted her head. "You know they invented texting for this, right?"

Emma chuckled. "Texting doesn't leave glitter on the kitchen table."

"Exactly," Lizzy said, taking a seat. "That's the point." Emma laughed softly. "Some things are worth the sparkle."

She dipped her pen again and continued writing. "Dear Linda... thinking of you and hoping this season brings you peace." She paused for a moment before sealing the envelope, her expression wistful.

Lizzy glanced up from her phone. "You okay?"

Emma smiled, but it was the quiet kind. "Just thinking how long it's been since I've seen some of these friends. We used to get together every December. Time just... moves differently now."

Lizzy looked at her mom's neat handwriting and the tiny stack of addressed envelopes, then down at her own phone where she was halfway through sending a funny reindeer meme to her best friend.

"Well," she said softly, "you're still sending them love. It just takes longer to get there."

Emma's smile widened. "Exactly. Every word is like a little visit."

Lizzy thought about that for a moment, then grinned. "I'm visiting digitally."

"I suppose that counts," Emma teased.

They worked side by side for a while—Emma with her pen, Lizzy with her phone. Every so often, they shared bits of conversation: Lizzy showing her mom a silly photo, Emma reading a line aloud to make sure it sounded right.

"Who's that one for?" Lizzy asked, pointing to a card with silver snowflakes.

"An old friend from college," Emma said. "We used to

stay up way too late watching movies and eating popcorn. Now we just trade cards and recipes."

Lizzy smiled. "That's kind of sweet."

Emma nodded. "It is. Some friendships just change shape over time."

Emma put her pen down in a moment of reflection realizing her daughter had become her friend. Emptiness in her heart flooded with happiness as she embraced the time with her daughter.

Lizzy finished sending her last message and set her phone down. "You know," she said quietly, "I could help you with the stamps."

Emma looked up in pleasant surprise. "You'd do that?"

Lizzy grinned. "Sure. It's the least I can do for the woman single-handedly keeping the postal service alive."

Emma laughed. "Very funny."

They worked together sealing envelopes, the sound of tape and paper mixing with the hum of holiday music. When they finished, Emma placed the stack neatly on the counter.

"Want to drop them at the mailbox with me?" she asked.

Lizzy hesitated, then shrugged. "Yeah. Why not."

Outside, the air was cool and clear. They slipped the letters into the red mailbox one by one, the final envelope sliding in with a soft thunk.

Lizzy smiled, watching them disappear. "Kind of satisfying," she admitted.

Emma nodded. "It always is."

As they walked back to the house, their hands brushed once, and neither of them moved away.

REFLECTION: Whether it's ink on paper or words on a screen, what matters most is the love we send out and who we take the time to reach.

Mother's Note: Do you feel like electronics can sometimes enhance or diminish your relationship with your daughter and others? What obstacles can you eliminate to break down these barriers?

_____

_____

_____

_____

Daughter's Note: What benefits do you experience from chatting in person that you would not receive over a text message?

_____

_____

_____

_____

DAY 12 – WINTER LIGHTS AND LATE TALKS

The night was crisp and still, the kind of cold that made every sound seem softer. The neighborhood glowed with a hundred tiny colors—rooftops strung with gold, porches lined with red and green, and the faint smell of wood smoke curling in the air.

Emma zipped up her coat. "Come on, walk with me. The lights are better after dark."

Lizzy looked up from her phone. "You say that every year."

Emma smiled. "And every year, I'm right."

Lizzy grinned and slipped her phone into her pocket. "Fine. But if I turn into an icicle, I'm haunting you."

"Deal," Emma said, laughing.

They walked side by side down the quiet street. The snow crunched softly beneath their boots, and the trees above glittered with ice like they'd been dusted in diamonds. Every few houses, Lizzy stopped to snap a photo—sometimes for her friends, sometimes just because she couldn't help it.

One yard had a glowing archway of lights shaped like candy canes. Emma paused under it, her breath visible in the cold. "You used to run through these when you were little," she said, smiling at the memory. "You'd pretend it was a magic tunnel."

Lizzy laughed. "That makes sense, I was dramatic even then."

Emma chuckled. "Still are."

They kept walking until they reached the park at the end of the block. The frozen pond shimmered under the lamplight, and the world felt suspended in calm. Emma pulled her scarf tighter.

"I always forget how beautiful this part of December is," she said quietly. "Before the rush, before the noise. Just... this."

Lizzy nodded, her tone softer now. "Yeah. It's kind of nice."

They sat on a cold bench, their breaths mingling in the frosty air.

"You know," Emma said, "when I was your age, I used to walk out here with Grandma. She'd stop and look at the lights, even when we saw the same ones every year. I never understood why she loved it so much."

Lizzy tilted her head. "And now you do?"

Emma smiled faintly. "I think so. I think it's about remembering that some beauty never really changes— even when everything else does."

Lizzy watched her mom for a moment, then looked out at the pond. "I guess that's kind of comforting."

Emma nodded. "It is."

They sat quietly for a while, not needing to fill the silence. The lights reflected in the ice like tiny stars scattered just for them.

After a long moment, Lizzy spoke again. "You know... my friends texted earlier. They were going to see the downtown lights. But... I think I like it better here."

Emma looked at her, surprised and touched. "Yeah?"

Lizzy shrugged, smiling shyly. "Yeah. The company's not bad."

Emma laughed, that warm, familiar sound that always made Lizzy smile. "I'll take it."

They started back home, brushing shoulders as they walked beneath the streetlights. The air was cold, but it didn't feel that way.

REFLECTION: The best lights aren't always the brightest ones, they're the ones that glow quietly, reminding us that we're never walking alone.

Mother: How do you feel you could incorporate more quality time with your daughter? Do you find it hard to articulate how you feel about the struggles of life and growing up with her?

_____

_____

_____

_____

Daughter: Is there something that help you open up more freely to your mom about your emotions and daily struggles? If you could say one thing to her know that was safe to put on paper, what would that be?

_____

_____

_____

_____

DAY 13 – THE GIFT LIST

The afternoon sun slanted through the kitchen window, glinting off a pile of tape dispensers and shiny red paper. Emma moved quickly, humming under her breath as she sorted gifts into neat piles.

"Okay," she said, flipping through her notebook. "Aunt Linda, check. The Donnellys, check. The Hendersons—oh, we still need their card."

Lizzy appeared in the doorway, one earbud still in, texting furiously. "Mom, you've been at this for hours. Can't you just do gift cards like a normal person?"

Emma smiled patiently. "Gift cards don't smell like cinnamon and effort."

Lizzy snorted. "Effort smells like tape and stress."

Emma laughed. "That's the holiday spirit."

She handed her daughter a roll of wrapping paper.

"Here, help me with these before your friends' movie night."

Lizzy groaned, glancing at the time on her phone. She saw the text from Sophie saying, *"Movie night at my house, all our favs, starting at 7. See ya soon!"*

Lizzy then turned to her mom, "Mom, they're already waiting for me."

"I know, sweetheart," Emma said gently, "but I could use an extra pair of hands."

Lizzy sighed but set her phone down, sitting at the table with exaggerated drama. "Fine. But this better be quick."

Emma grinned. "Speed wrapping. My favorite kind."

They worked side by side—sort of. Emma folded edges neatly; Lizzy wrestled the paper like it had personally offended her.

"Mom," Lizzy said, laughing despite herself, "you're wrapping like it's a contest."

"It is," Emma said. "Against the clock—and gravity."

Lizzy shook her head, smiling. "You're impossible."

They kept working, the sound of paper crinkling filling the room. Lizzy's texts buzzed again, and she paused, half reaching for her phone, then hesitating. She looked at her mom, humming softly as she tied a bow on a gift labeled To Grandma, Love Always.

Something about that moment—the smell of cocoa, the low hum of music, the way the lights flickered on the tree—made her stop.

"Who's that one for?" Lizzy asked, pointing to a small box.

Emma smiled. "Our neighbor, Mrs. Jensen. She's alone this year, so I thought she'd like something to open."

Lizzy frowned slightly, then picked up a roll of ribbon. "That's really nice."

Emma shrugged, tying another knot. "Sometimes people just need to know they're remembered."

They wrapped in silence for a bit, the rush softening into rhythm.

When the last bow was tied, Lizzy leaned back, surveying the chaos of ribbons and paper bits. "We actually finished," she said, surprised.

Emma exhaled, smiling. "See? Magic."

Lizzy grinned. "More like manual labor."

Emma laughed. "Maybe. But look what we did together."

Lizzy glanced at her phone, then turned it face down. "Yeah," she said quietly. "It's... actually kind of nice."

Emma met her eyes. "You can still go meet your friends."

Lizzy nodded her head and brought back out her phone, "I'll meet you outside" she wrote to Sophie excitedly.

She turned to her mom and asked, "are you sure you'll be ok without me?"

Emma's eyes softened, "yes go have fun".

Lizzy turned to her mom before she went out the day stopping to say, "thanks mom, it was a good day".

Emma smiled as she treasured their time together and for the first time all day, the rush slowed into something that felt like peace.

Reflection: The holidays move fast but the ones we slow down for are the ones that stay.

Mother's Note: Do you feel like you have trouble slowing down to enjoy the moments and relationships in your life? Are there times you feel alone as your daughter grows up and expands her relationships beyond her family? How do you feel you can make the moments count when you are together?

_____

_____

_____

Daughter's Note: Do you ever have mixed emotions about spending time with friends versus your family? Do you sometimes find it easier to talk to friends about difficult subjects? What subjects would you like to talk about with your mom, but are unable to?

_____

_____

_____

DAY 14 – MOVIE NIGHT

The smell of buttery popcorn filled the living room as Emma arranged blankets and fluffed the couch pillows. The tree lights flickered softly in the background, casting tiny reflections across the room.

"Movie night!" she called. "I'll make the snacks; you pick the movie."

Lizzy appeared with two mugs of cocoa and a mischievous grin. "Already done. We're watching Holiday Rush. Don't worry, it's festive and romantic."

Emma smiled politely. "You mean the one where everyone falls in love in the middle of a snowstorm?"

Lizzy gasped. "That's basically every Christmas movie, Mom."

"Exactly my point," Emma teased, reaching into her tote bag and holding up a DVD case. "Or... we could watch White Christmas."

Lizzy groaned. "You've got to be kidding me. Mom, that movie is ancient."

"Classic," Emma corrected. "There's a difference."

"Only to people who remember rotary phones."

Emma feigned offense. "I'll have you know, Bing Crosby paved the way for your modern-day romantic comedies."

Lizzy smirked. "Pretty sure Netflix did that."

They both laughed, but beneath it was the familiar spark of mother-daughter tug-of-war — love wrapped in eye-rolling patience.

Emma waved her hand. "Fine, compromise: we'll start with mine, then yours."

"Deal," Lizzy said, curling up on the couch with the blanket. "But if there's singing every two minutes, I'm muting it."

The first movie began. Black-and-white snow fell across the screen, and Emma hummed along softly to the opening song.

Lizzy shifted, trying to stay interested, but halfway through she was glancing at her phone.

Emma caught her. "You can text if you want," she said gently.

Lizzy sighed. "No, I'm watching. It's just... slow."

Emma smiled faintly. "It's okay. I used to think the same thing when Grandma made me watch it."

That made Lizzy pause. "Really?"

Emma nodded. "And now, every time I hear this song,

I remember sitting beside her — cocoa in one hand, her arm around me, both of us pretending we weren't crying at the ending."

Lizzy set her phone down quietly. "She'd probably like that we're watching it."

Emma's voice softened. "Yeah. I think she would."

They sat together in silence for a while — not the uncomfortable kind, but the kind that felt full.

When the movie ended, Emma started to reach for the remote, but Lizzy stopped her. "You can leave it on," she said softly. "I'll survive another song or two."

Emma smiled, surprised but touched. "Okay, your turn next."

Lizzy cued up her movie — a colorful, fast-talking holiday rom-com — and they watched in comfortable contrast: Emma chuckling at the dialogue she didn't quite follow, Lizzy laughing at all the predictable moments she swore she hated.

By the time the credits rolled, neither had moved for a long time.

Lizzy yawned, setting her empty cocoa mug on the coffee table. "So... your movie wasn't terrible."

Emma smiled sleepily. "And yours wasn't too bad."

Lizzy laughed. "High praise."

They shared a grin — the kind that said more than words.

Emma shifted under the blanket. "You cold?"

Lizzy shook her head. "No. Just... tired."

"Come here," Emma whispered. Lizzy quickly got into the covers and snuggled her feet next to her mom to get warm. The room was quiet except for the faint hum of the TV, still playing softly — one more song drifting into the night.

Emma brushed a strand of hair from her daughter's face. "You know," she murmured, "this is my favorite part of the holidays."

Lizzy smiled, eyes already heavy. "What is?"

"This," Emma said softly. "Right here."

Within minutes, Lizzy was asleep, her breathing even, the flicker of the tree lights dancing across both of their faces.

Emma stayed awake just long enough to whisper, "Merry almost Christmas, sweetheart," before closing her eyes too.

REFLECTION: Sometimes peace doesn't come from agreeing on everything, it comes from simply being there when the world goes quiet.

Mother's Note: In what instances, could compromise be beneficial? Do you find compromise to be difficult? If so, why?

_____

_____

_____

_____

Daughter's Note: When do you think it's a good idea to compromise when it comes to relationships such as your mother or other friends?

_____

_____

_____

_____

DAY 15 – SNOW DAY SURPRISES

*T*he next morning, Emma woke to the quiet hush that only fresh snow brings. For a moment, she stayed still, her daughter's head resting against her shoulder, the soft glow of daylight filtering through the curtains.

Then came the unmistakable sound of the furnace kicking on—and the sudden realization that she had not planned for this much snow.

She eased out from under the blanket and peeked through the window. The world outside was completely white. Driveway gone. Mailbox buried. A lopsided snowman from last week standing heroically up to his chin in powder.

"Lizzy," she said softly. "Wake up."

Lizzy groaned. "No. Five more minutes."

"School's canceled."

Lizzy's eyes flew open. "Seriously?"

Emma nodded. "Snow day."

Lizzy grinned, stretching. "Best words ever."

They shuffled into the kitchen, still in pajamas. Emma started cocoa while Lizzy raided the fridge.

"Do we have waffles?"

"Nope."

"Bagels?"

"Also nope."

Lizzy frowned. "We're out of everything?"

Emma smiled. "We were supposed to grocery shop yesterday."

Lizzy sighed. "The chaos begins."

They made cinnamon toast instead—one slice burnt, one perfect—and ate by the window, watching the steady snowfall.

"So, what's the plan?" Lizzy asked, spreading jam. "Blanket fort? Movie marathon? TikTok dance challenge?"

Emma laughed. "How about shoveling?"

Lizzy stared. "You can't say 'snow day' and 'shoveling' in the same sentence, Mom."

"I just did."

By late morning, chaos was in full swing. Boots by the door, gloves that didn't match, and one broken snow shovel later, they were both outside.

Emma worked in steady lines; Lizzy made a half-hearted attempt before abandoning her post to start rolling a snowball.

"Don't you dare throw that," Emma warned.

Lizzy grinned. "It's not for throwing—it's the base of my masterpiece."

Emma eyed her suspiciously. "Your masterpiece?"

"My next-level snowwoman."

Within minutes, their "project" had turned into a full-blown snow fight. Emma shrieked as snow flew past her scarf.

"Unfair!" she called. "You have longer arms!"

Lizzy laughed, breathless. "You're the one who said we needed exercise!"

They collapsed in the snow, cheeks red, laughing so hard they could barely breathe.

When they finally trudged back inside, the house was a scene of wet boots, puddles, and dripping mittens hanging over chairs.

Emma sighed. "Our poor floor."

Lizzy dropped onto the couch, still smiling. "Worth it."

Emma sat beside her, handing over a fresh mug of cocoa. "Completely."

They sipped in silence for a moment, their hair still damp, the room filled with the smell of chocolate and melting snow.

Lizzy looked at her mom and smiled. "You know, for a chaotic day, this turned out pretty perfect."

Emma nodded. "That's the funny thing about chaos —it usually comes with laughter."

Lizzy grinned. "And burnt toast."

Emma laughed. "Always."

The wind brushed softly against the windows, and for the rest of the day, they stayed tucked in—messy, happy, and exactly where they needed to be.

Reflection: Sometimes joy hides in the mess- the snow on the floor, the laughter between the shovels and the moments that don't go as planned.

Mother's Note: Do you find it hard to divert plans when you already have your schedule planned? Is there room to make quality time, in the midst of chaos?

_____

_____

_____

_____

Daughter's Note: Do you feel like you don't have time to relax when schedules are busy? What are ways you can try to unwind but also enjoy time with your family?

_____

_____

_____

_____

DAY 16 – THE ARGUMENT

The morning started with good intentions — a long list on the fridge and the smell of coffee drifting through the kitchen.

Emma stood in front of her planner, tapping a pen against the counter. "Okay," she muttered, "baking, cards, grocery run, gift wrapping, laundry..."

She glanced at the clock and sighed. "We're behind."

Lizzy shuffled in wearing slippers and a hoodie, phone in hand. "Behind on what?"

Emma gestured to the list. "Everything. If we want to get things done before Christmas Eve, we need to start now."

Lizzy frowned. "It's Saturday and it's not even ten, Mom. Can't we just chill for, like, one morning?"

"Chill?" Emma repeated. "Lizzy, the house looks like a wrapping paper factory exploded."

Lizzy rolled her eyes. "You're the one who wanted to handwrite Christmas cards."

"Because it's thoughtful," Emma snapped.

"Or exhausting," Lizzy muttered.

Emma froze, turning toward her. "Excuse me?"

Lizzy sighed, not meaning to sound sharp but too tired to smooth it out. "You stress about every little thing, Mom. Maybe Christmas doesn't have to be perfect."

Emma's voice rose before she could stop it. "You think I don't know that? You think I want to feel like I'm holding everything together by a thread?"

Lizzy blinked, startled. "That's not what I said—"

Emma ran a hand through her hair. "I just— I want things to feel special. For once. Like when you were little, when it wasn't all rushing and screens and—"

Lizzy cut in, voice tight. "Maybe I'm not a little kid anymore!"

The silence that followed was thick and stinging.

Emma looked away first. "Right. You're not." Her voice softened but broke around the edges. "I just thought maybe you'd want to spend some of it with me anyway."

Lizzy hesitated, guilt flickering — but frustration still burned hotter. "I do, Mom. But not like this. You're turning Christmas into homework."

The words landed heavier than she meant. Emma's shoulders stiffened. "Fine," she said quietly. "Go. Do whatever you want."

Lizzy's throat tightened. "I will."

The door to her room shut harder than either of them expected.

Hours passed in uneasy quiet.

Emma moved through the motions — folding laundry, wrapping gifts — each task done in silence. The radio played faintly, cheerful songs clashing with the heavy stillness of the house.

In her room, Lizzy lay on her bed, phone untouched, scrolling mindlessly. But every carol she heard through the walls made her stomach twist a little tighter.

Finally, Emma sat at the kitchen table, staring at the half-finished list. Her pen hovered over the page, but all she could think about was the look on her daughter's face — hurt, not angry.

She sighed, whispering to no one, "I just wanted to make it nice."

Upstairs, Lizzy stared at the ceiling, remembering the crack in her mom's voice. It wasn't about cookies or wrapping paper. It was about her trying — maybe too hard — to keep something beautiful alive.

Reflection: Sometimes love slips beneath the noise, waiting for the moment when we're ready to see it again.

Mother's Note: How do you feel after an argument? Are there things that can help you avoid getting frustrated over the holidays and in everyday life? Are you able to forgive yourself?

_____

_____

_____

_____

Daughter's Note: Do you feel like forgiveness is difficult? What emotions arise for you when there is an argument? What helps you feel better after a disagreement?

_____

_____

_____

_____

DAY 17 – GOING THROUGH THE MOTIONS

*T*he next morning came quietly, the kind of gray December light that felt heavy even through the curtains. The snow from yesterday had settled into soft drifts, muffling the world outside.

In the kitchen, Emma moved carefully, like noise itself might crack the fragile quiet. She made coffee, buttered toast, and glanced toward the hallway — no sound from Lizzy's room.

She checked the list on the fridge, but the words blurred together. Cookies. Laundry. Gifts. Cards. They all felt suddenly meaningless, little reminders of a joy she couldn't quite reach.

Upstairs, Lizzy sat on her bed, scrolling through her phone without seeing anything. The silence from downstairs pressed against her chest. She thought about going to help, about saying I'm sorry, but every time she imagined walking into the kitchen, her stomach knotted.

By midmorning, they were both pretending not to notice the other's distance.

Emma cleaned the counters that were already clean. Lizzy folded laundry that didn't really need folding. They moved through the same house like ghosts — connected by love, separated by pride.

At noon, Emma broke the silence. "There's soup on the stove," she said, not quite looking up.

"Thanks," Lizzy replied quietly.

They ate at separate times.

The house, usually full of music during this time of year, stayed still. The twinkle lights glowed dimly against the gray afternoon.

Later, as the day wore on, Emma found herself standing by the tree. The ornament Lizzy had fixed — the one that had meant so much — caught her eye. The light hit it just right, reflecting gold cracks that shimmered like tiny rivers.

Her throat tightened. She reached out to touch it but stopped short, her hand hovering just above the branch.

Upstairs, Lizzy sat cross-legged on the floor, wrapping a few gifts for friends. The sound of tape and paper filled the quiet. When she reached for a gift tag, her hand brushed against one that said To Mom. She stared at it for a long time. Then she tucked it back in the box, unfinished. Evening settled slowly. Emma stood at the sink, watching the snow fall outside. The reflection of the tree lights shimmered against the window — a thousand tiny stars she couldn't quite feel.

In her room, Lizzy sat by the glow of her phone, watching old photos pop up — summers at the lake, cookie-baking days, Christmas mornings when everything had felt easy. Her chest ached with missing something she didn't even realize they still had.

She almost went downstairs. Almost.

But not yet.

The house stayed quiet, both caught in the stillness — each waiting for the other to make the first move.

Reflection: Some days aren't about fixing what's broken, there are about sitting in the quiet long enough to remember why it matters.

Mother's Note: Do you feel like issues can be resolved after a disagreement? What lessons have you learned from your daughter about moving forward and forgiveness?

_____

_____

_____

_____

Daughter's Note: How do you recover from a disagreement with friends and family? What has your mom taught you about loving unconditionally?

_____

_____

_____

_____

DAY 18 – SMALL STEPS

The next morning arrived with sunlight — pale and thin, but enough to make the snow outside glisten again. The house was still quiet, but the stillness felt different today. Not heavy. Just waiting.

Emma stirred her coffee absentmindedly, the spoon tapping the side of the mug in a slow rhythm. She had barely slept. The argument replayed over and over in her head — each word, each sigh. She picked up the wooden advent calendar hoping there was some magic that might cure this tension with Lizzy. Day 17, read, "Have Hope".

She glanced at the fridge, where yesterday's list still hung crookedly. Without really thinking, she pulled it down and folded it in half. Maybe today didn't need a list. Maybe it just needed... breathing room.

Upstairs, Lizzy lay under her blanket, scrolling aimlessly through her messages. A few texts from friends blinked at the top of her screen — plans, jokes, invitations — but she didn't respond. Her thoughts kept wandering to the sound of her mom's voice, the way it had cracked when she said, *I just wanted to make it nice.*

Her chest ached.

She slipped out of bed and padded down the hallway. When she reached the stairs, she hesitated. The smell of coffee drifted up — familiar, comforting.

Lizzy hovered for a moment before turning toward the kitchen.

Emma looked up from the sink, surprised. "Morning," she said softly.

Lizzy nodded. "Morning." She moved to the counter, opening the cabinet for a mug. "We're out of the peppermint creamer."

Emma smiled faintly. "I know. I forgot to buy more."

"I can walk to the corner store later," Lizzy said.

Emma's hand paused midair, then lowered. "That would be nice. Thank you."

It wasn't much — but it was something.

They stood there for a moment in the warm, quiet kitchen. Lizzy poured her cocoa, and Emma handed her the spoon without a word. Their fingers brushed, just barely, but it was enough to make them both glance up and smile awkwardly.

The rest of the day moved gently.

Emma started wrapping gifts at the dining table. Lizzy joined after a while, pulling a chair close but not saying anything. She reached for the tape when her mom couldn't find it, cut ribbons, folded paper — both moving carefully, like rebuilding something delicate.

Every so often, Emma would hum softly along to the radio. Lizzy didn't comment, but she didn't put her earbuds in either.

By late afternoon, the table was covered in half-wrapped boxes, stray ribbons, and empty cocoa mugs.

Lizzy stretched and looked at the mess. "Guess we're not professional wrappers after all."

Emma smiled. "We've got heart. That's close enough."

Lizzy smirked. "And glitter. Everywhere."

They both laughed, quietly at first, but real.

For the first time in two days, it didn't feel like pretending.

That night, as Emma tidied the kitchen, she found a small note stuck to the fridge:

"I'll get the peppermint creamer tomorrow. Love, M."

She smiled, touching the paper gently before tucking it next to a photo of them from a few Christmases ago — Lizzy missing her front teeth, Emma mid-laugh, both faces glowing.

Upstairs, Lizzy lay in bed, staring at the faint reflection of the Christmas lights outside her window. She didn't know if things were fixed yet. But they felt... softer.

And for now, that was enough.

Reflection: Healing rarely begins with big speeches; sometimes it's a shared silence, a small gesture, or a note left behind, remembering how to speak again.

Mother's Note: What steps can you take, in your own life, to help you heal from past experiences and loss?

_____

_____

_____

_____

Daughter's Note: What things help you heal most? How can you incorporate those more into your life?

_____

_____

_____

_____

DAY 19 – PEPPERMINT AND APOLOGIES

Snow flurries drifted lazily past the window as the morning light spread across the kitchen. The house still carried yesterday's calm — quiet, tentative, but warm.

Emma was stirring oatmeal on the stove when she heard the sound of boots near the door.

Lizzy came in, cheeks flushed from the cold, a paper bag in her arms. "Mission accomplished," she said, holding up a familiar red-and-white bottle. "They had one left."

Emma turned, surprised and smiling before she could stop herself. "You actually went?"

Lizzy grinned. "I promised, didn't I?"

Emma took the bottle from her, brushing a bit of snow off the cap. "You didn't have to."

"I wanted to," Lizzy said softly.

For a moment, they stood in the kitchen — mother and daughter, the faint smell of cinnamon and winter air between them.

"Do you want some?" Emma asked, already reaching for another mug.

Lizzy nodded. "Always."

Emma poured two cups of coffee, adding a generous swirl of peppermint creamer to each. The scent filled the room, sweet and familiar. She slid one mug across the counter toward her daughter.

Lizzy smiled, taking it carefully. "You always make it taste better."

"That's because I use the good mug," Emma said with a wink.

They both laughed, and the sound came easily this time — soft but full.

They drank in silence for a while, the clinking of spoons and the hum of the heater the only sounds between them.

Then, without planning to, Lizzy said, "I'm sorry."

Emma looked up. "For what?"

Lizzy shrugged, eyes on her mug. "For what I said the other day. About Christmas being too much. I didn't mean it like that. I just... didn't understand."

Emma's voice softened. "Understand what?"

"That you do all of this because you care," Lizzy said. "You're not trying to make it perfect. You're trying to make it matter."

Emma's throat tightened. "Oh, sweetheart..." She reached across the counter, covering Lizzy's hand with hers. "I shouldn't have yelled. You were right — I was trying too hard."

Lizzy smiled faintly. "Maybe we both were."

They sat quietly for a moment, the silence gentle now. The kind that felt safe again.

Emma exhaled, a small laugh escaping. "You know, your grandma used to say peppermint was a cure for everything."

Lizzy grinned. "Even guilt?"

"Especially guilt," Emma said, raising her mug.

Lizzy clinked hers against it. "Then cheers to that."

They both laughed — light, real, healing.

As the snow continued to fall outside, Emma thought about how easily love could break, and how beautifully it could mend — not through grand gestures, but through small, peppermint-scented mornings like this.

Reflection: Forgiveness does not always need words. Sometimes it arrives in the form of warm coffee, small laughter and the simple act of showing up again.

Mother's Note: What little things does your daughter do, that make you appreciate her as a person. How could you show her that you appreciate her actions more?

_____

_____

_____

_____

Daughter's Note: In what ways do you need others to show you love (i.e. through actions, words, gifts)? How do you think you could show your love to her in a way that your mom might recognize?

_____

_____

_____

_____

DAY 20 – THE CHRISTMAS MARKET

The air smelled like roasted chestnuts and cinnamon sugar. Strings of lights crisscrossed overhead, glowing against the pale winter sky. The local Christmas market was alive with the hum of laughter, the jingling of bells, and the sound of carolers somewhere near the center square.

Emma and Lizzy walked side by side through the crowd, their breath visible in the cold. It was the first time all week that the weight between them felt completely gone.

Lizzy tugged her scarf tighter. "You really picked the coldest day of the year for this."

Emma smiled. "Tradition builds character."

"Frostbite builds trauma," Lizzy muttered playfully.

Emma laughed. "You'll survive."

They passed a booth selling handmade ornaments.

Lizzy stopped, drawn to one shaped like a glass heart streaked with gold. She turned it in her glove, the light catching its delicate cracks.

"Look," she said. "It's like the one we fixed.

Emma's eyes softened. "It really is."

Lizzy smiled. "We should get it—like, a matching one. Keeps the theme going."

Emma nodded. "That's a lovely idea."

They bought it, both pretending not to notice how much it meant.

The market grew busier as the afternoon went on. Emma spotted a familiar face at a booth selling wreaths —an old friend from her book club. "Oh my goodness, Diane!" she exclaimed, waving.

Diane turned, her face lighting up. "Emma! It's been ages!"

The two women hugged tightly, laughter spilling into the air as they caught up. Lizzy hung back a little, sipping her cocoa, watching how easily her mom glowed when she was surrounded by people who'd known her for years. There was something steady in that, something comforting.

Emma checked her phone to see if her friends had reached the market yet, as she was anxious to spend time with familiar faces.

Not far away, a burst of laughter broke out near the cider stand. "Lizzy!"

She turned to see her friends—Sophie, Bella, and Ava

—waving her over, bundled in bright scarves and clutching bags of cookies and cocoa.

Emma saw the hesitation flicker across her daughter's face and smiled. "Go ahead. I'll be right over there," she said, nodding toward the carolers by the fountain.

Lizzy smiled gratefully and jogged toward her friends, her breath puffing in the air.

"Finally!" Sophie laughed. "We thought you were hibernating!"

"I was on family duty," Lizzy teased, rolling her eyes—but smiling. "Apparently, it's character building."

The girls wandered between stalls, sharing bites of gingerbread and stories from school. For the first time in days, Lizzy felt fully in her own world again—light, effortless, connected.

A few booths away, Emma and Diane stood under a string of golden lights, talking about everything and nothing—the kind of friendship that survives through seasons.

"It's nice to see you smiling again," Diane said kindly.

Emma smiled. "Yeah... it's been a rough week. But she and I are getting there."

Diane squeezed her hand. "You're both growing. That's what this time of year does—it reminds us what still matters."

Emma looked over Diane's shoulder and saw Lizzy with her friends, laughing, carefree. Her heart softened.

Different circles, she thought. Same joy.

When Lizzy returned, cheeks pink from the cold, Emma was waiting by the fountain. The carolers were finishing a song—O Holy Night—their voices rising pure and steady in the cold air.

Lizzy slipped her arm through her mother's.

Emma smiled. "Did you have fun?"

"Yeah," Lizzy said. "You?"

"I did," Emma said, glancing toward where Diane stood waving goodbye. "We both found our people, didn't we?"

Lizzy laughed. "Guess we did."

The final note of the carol rose into the night, and for a moment, everything felt suspended—the lights, the music, the quiet between them.

They didn't say anything else, but they didn't need to.

They walked back toward the market's edge, two different worlds side by side—mother and daughter, each learning how to belong in their own way, and still somehow belonging most right there together.

REFLECTION: The magic of the holidays isn't found in one place or tradition; it's in the way connection threads through all of them, no matter the age or circle.

Mother's Note: What is your experience in relationships with other women? What are you teaching your daughter about relationships with people and other women?

_____

_____

_____

_____

Daughter's Note: What is your relationship with friends? Would you like a stronger bond with your mother and other friends in your life? How could you work to make these relationships more meaningful?

_____

_____

_____

_____

DAY 21 – THE VISITOR

Snow began again in the early evening—slow, soft flakes drifting past the windows. The house hummed faintly with the sound of the heater, and Emma stood in the kitchen kneading cookie dough, trying to ignore the drip-drip-drip from the upstairs bathroom ceiling.

She sighed, glancing up. "Not tonight," she whispered.

Lizzy, sitting at the table sketching holiday cards, looked up. "It's leaking again?"

Emma nodded, wiping her hands on a towel. "Pipe's been stubborn for weeks. I called the plumber twice, but everyone's booked till after Christmas."

Lizzy nodded to her mom in agreement and then opened the next day on the Advent Calendar that lay beside the holiday cards. She read it aloud "Just Believe".

"These days are funny, just two words she thought. What does that even mean" Lizzy said as they continued their holiday cards.

Before she could say more, headlights swept briefly across the snow-covered window, followed by the crunch of tires in the driveway.

Emma frowned. "Who'd be out in this?"

When she opened the door, a gust of cold air swept in —and with it, a woman bundled in a heavy coat, snowflakes clinging to her scarf.

"Emma?"

It took her a moment to recognize the voice. "Clara?"

The woman smiled, weary but warm. "Surprise. I know it's been forever—I was driving through town to go see my brother, and my car decided it doesn't like winter anymore."

Emma blinked, stunned. Clara had been one of her closest friends years ago, they'd taught at the same school, swapped baby photos, shared late-night calls after loss. Life, as it always did, had stretched the distance.

"Come in, come in!" Emma said quickly. "You must be freezing."

Inside, the three of them crowded near the heater while Emma made cocoa. Clara's cheeks were pink, her curls damp from snow.

"You look exactly the same," Emma said with a smile.

Clara laughed. "I look exhausted."

"You always did, even when you weren't," Emma teased.

Lizzy hovered nearby, curious. "How do you two know each other?"

Clara smiled at her. "Your mom and I used to run the school winter fair together. She baked; I organized. We were chaos and glitter in equal measure."

Lizzy grinned. "Sounds about right."

Just then, the familiar drip-drip echoed from upstairs again. Emma sighed. "That's the ceiling. Ignore it; I've tried everything."

Clara tilted her head, listening. "You sure it's not a loose valve? I had that exact sound last winter."

Emma frowned. "Loose valve?"

Clara set her mug down. "Got a wrench?"

Within minutes, the two women were halfway up the stairs, flashlights in hand, laughing like the years had melted away. Lizzy followed, half amused, half amazed.

Clara knelt beside the bathroom cabinet, sleeves rolled up. "There's your culprit," she said, tightening a small silver piece. "You were one drip away from a disaster."

Emma shook her head in disbelief. "You're telling me you came here stranded and fixed my house?"

Clara laughed. "Occupational hazard of being a handy widow with too many tools in her trunk."

Lizzy burst out laughing. "You're officially my hero."

"Add it to my résumé," Clara said, tightening one last bolt.

Back downstairs, the three of them sat by the fireplace, steam curling from their cocoa mugs. The storm pressed softly against the windows, but the house finally felt warm in more ways than one.

Emma leaned back, smiling. "You always did have perfect timing."

Clara sipped her cocoa. "Funny thing is, I thought I was the one who needed help tonight."

Emma tilted her head. "And you ended up helping us."

Clara smiled, eyes shining in the firelight. "That's how friendship works, isn't it? We just take turns."

Lizzy watched them—these two women, both strong in quiet ways, laughing over old stories about classroom disasters, burnt cookies, and the year they almost froze running a school fair booth in the snow.

She saw something in them she hadn't noticed before: not just history, but kinship. A reflection of what she had with her own mom—different, older, but made of the same thread.

As the night deepened, the three of them curled up under blankets, the fire popping softly.

Clara glanced toward the ceiling. "No drips."

Emma smiled. "Not a sound."

Lizzy yawned. "You should move in. We clearly need supervision."

Clara laughed. "I'll send my rates in gingerbread cookies."

When they finally said goodnight, Emma paused at the bottom of the stairs. "Clara?"

"Yeah?"

"Thank you. For showing up. For... everything."

Clara's smile was quiet and knowing. "You would've done the same for me."

Emma nodded, voice soft. "Always."

As the house settled into sleep, Emma stood by the doorway for a moment, watching the snow fall again— thinking about how help, love, and grace often arrive not when we expect them, but exactly when we need them.

REFLECTION: Sometimes the people who need saving are the ones that end up saving us-reminding us that love, in all its forms, is a circle that never stops coming back around.

Mother's Note: Has there been influential people in your life that have shaped you as a person? In what ways do you emulate those positive aspects?

_____

_____

_____

_____

Daughter's Note: What relationships would you like to have in your life and which ones would you like to avoid? Do you feel the current relationships you have are valuable ones that give as much to the relationship as you currently give? If not, how could you change this.

_____

_____

_____

_____

DAY 22 – THE LETTER

The snow had stopped sometime in the night, leaving the world blanketed and still. Sunlight filtered through frosted glass, laying soft gold stripes across the living room floor.

Emma woke to the hush of a house at peace, no dripping ceiling, no storm rattling the windows. The quiet felt earned.

She slipped downstairs, still in her robe, smiling at the sight of Clara's empty mug neatly washed on the counter. But when she looked closer, she noticed an envelope beneath it — folded once, her name written across the front in Clara's handwriting.

Thanks for the warmth and the laughter, dear friend. The road cleared early. I fixed the latch on the back door, too. Merry Christmas, Em.

Emma smiled softly, shaking her head. "That woman

never could sit still."

She reached for her coffee mug — and that's when she saw it.

Tucked into a branch of the Christmas tree, half-hidden behind a silver ribbon, was another envelope — cream paper edged in faint gold.

The handwriting stopped her cold.

Her mother's.

The room seemed to tilt. She walked over, almost afraid to touch it.

The name on the front read:

To Emma — *For the Christmas You Will Need It Most*

Footsteps padded down the stairs.

"Mom?" Lizzy's voice was sleepy but warm. "You're up early."

Emma turned, still holding the letter. Her voice trembled. "Sweetheart... come here."

Lizzy sat beside her on the couch, tucking her legs under a blanket. "What's that?"

Emma swallowed hard. "It's from Grandma."

Lizzy's eyes widened. "Wait — like from before she passed?"

Emma nodded. "I must've packed it away years ago. But... I've never seen this one."

She unfolded it slowly. The scent that rose from the paper was faint but familiar — cedar, sugar, and something softer, something like memory.

Emma's voice was barely above a whisper as she began to read aloud:

My Dearest Girl,

There will come a time at Christmas when your hands are tired from holding everything together. You'll wonder if you've done enough, if the magic is slipping through your fingers.

Remember: Christmas was never about perfect trees or polished smiles. It's about hearts trying, even when they're a little cracked. It's about passing the light forward.

You'll know it's time when you see the spark in someone else's eye-maybe your own child's-and you'll realize you've already done enough. You've made it shine.

And if you need a reminder...look for the letter. You'll find it when you're ready.

All my love, Always
-Mom

Emma's hand trembled. The words blurred.

Lizzy leaned closer, resting her head gently against her mother's shoulder. "She knew," she whispered. "She knew you'd need it."

Emma nodded, tears catching the light. "I think she did."

For a moment, neither spoke. The world seemed to hold its breath — just the hum of the heater, the faint scent of cinnamon and snow.

Then Lizzy reached out and touched the letter with her fingertips. "You know what's crazy?" she said softly. "Grandma's words... they sound like you."

Emma smiled through her tears. "I used to think I was trying to live up to her. Maybe I've just been continuing her."

Lizzy's eyes glistened. "And one day... maybe I'll continue you."

Emma looked at her daughter — really looked — and saw her mother's spark there, quiet and bright and alive.

She exhaled a laugh that sounded like both grief and grace. "Then I'd say your grandmother's magic did its job."

Lizzy smiled. "It's still doing it."

They placed the letter back among the branches, nestled between the golden heart ornament and a tiny angel made from lace. Emma lit a single candle beneath it. The flame flickered once, then steadied.

Lizzy whispered, "Do you think Grandma sent Clara here?"

Emma smiled softly. "I think love finds its way — through storms, through friends, through time."

Lizzy leaned into her. "Then I hope I learn how to send it forward, too."

Emma kissed the top of her head. "You already are."

Outside, the snow began again — soft and certain — while inside, three generations of love seemed to shimmer in the candlelight.

REFLECTION: Love doesn't end. It echoes through letters, through laughter, through quiet courage of those who keep the light going.

Mother's Note: In what ways has your mother, or another influential woman, impacted your relationship with your own daughter? What lesson is important from your past that could help your future relationship with your daughter?

_____

_____

_____

_____

Daughter's Note: Who inspires you to live authentically? Do you feel like there is one person that has helped you through a difficult time?

_____

_____

_____

_____

DAY 23 – THE STAR

he day began in a hush of white light, the snow outside so bright it seemed to glow from within. Inside, the house felt calm — not quiet like absence, but quiet like peace.

Emma opened the next day on the calendar, realizing how close it was to Christmas. Day 23 read, "The Star shines bright". Beautiful sentiment she thought as she continued with cleaning the kitchen from the night before.

Lizzy was the first to notice the letter still resting beneath the tree. She picked it up carefully, tracing the edges as if it might disappear.

"Mom," she called softly, "can we do something for Grandma? Something ... to keep her close?"

Emma paused, dish towel in hand. "What do you have in mind?"

Lizzy shrugged. "Something we make. Together."

Emma smiled. "Then we'll make it shine."

By midday the dining table had become a small universe of craft paper, glue, and ribbon. They worked side by side — Lizzy cutting, Emma smoothing, both humming the same carol under their breath. When they finished, the star shimmered softly in the winter light: bits of gold foil, lace from an old curtain, and a bead from Emma's wedding dress.

"It's crooked," Lizzy said, laughing.

Emma smiled. "Then it's honest."

They placed the star near the top of the tree, beside the glass angel that had once been her mother's. For a moment, the two decorations caught the same slant of sunlight and glowed so brightly that the whole room seemed to breathe.

"Did you see that?" Lizzy whispered.

Emma blinked. "It must be the reflection ... from the window."

Lizzy shook her head. "There isn't any sun anymore."

They turned toward the window. Clouds had already rolled in, soft gray against the late-day sky. But the star still shimmered, pulsing faintly, gold and white and alive.

Neither spoke. The house was utterly still — the kind of stillness that makes you aware of your own heartbeat.

Then the air changed. The scent of cedar and sugar — the same as the letter — drifted faintly through the room.

Emma's eyes widened. "Do you ... smell that?"

Lizzy nodded slowly. "It's her."

The light from the star flared once, then softened into a warm glow that lingered just long enough for them both to feel it — a quiet pulse of something loving, familiar, and beyond explanation.

Lizzy reached for her mother's hand. Neither of them looked away.

After a long moment, the glow dimmed, leaving only the gentle twinkle of the tree lights.

Emma exhaled, tears brimming. "Maybe it was the candle," she said softly, though her voice didn't sound convinced.

Lizzy squeezed her hand. "Or maybe it was exactly what it looked like."

Emma smiled through the tears. "Maybe some miracles don't need to be proven. Maybe they just need to be seen."

They stood there together, the handmade star gleaming faintly above them, the air still humming with something they could both feel but not name.

That night, before bed, Lizzy tucked the letter beside her nightstand. "Do you think Grandma really saw us today?" she asked sleepily.

Emma smoothed her hair. "I think she never stopped."

Outside, snow began to fall again — soft, slow, endless — as the little star over the tree shimmered one last time, steady and sure against the dark.

REFLECTION: A miracle isn't always thunder and trumpets. Sometimes it's the quiet shimmer that stays in your heart long after the light fades.

Mother's Note: Is there a special moment that only you and your daughter share? What is it and how does it make your relationship special?

_____

_____

_____

_____

Daughter's Note: Is there a memory of your mom that you cherish? Describe how that memory and others, make your relationship special?

_____

_____

_____

_____

DAY 24 – CHRISTMAS EVE

*E*vening wrapped the town in silver hush. Snow fell soft as breath, and the house glowed like a lantern against the dark.

Emma stirred cocoa on the stove while Lizzy strung popcorn on thread. The air smelled of cinnamon, candle wax, and something peaceful that hadn't visited in years.

Lizzy pushed open the door of Day 24 of the advent calendar. "Miracles of the season shine bright". She was so busy getting the day started, she hadn't even read the writing.

They'd spent the day baking, laughing, remembering. Everything felt lighter, as if the miracle of the night before still shimmered unseen in the corners.

A knock came at the door.

When Emma opened it, Clara stood there again — cheeks flushed from the cold, curls dusted with snow.

"You didn't think I'd miss Christmas Eve, did you?" she said, holding up a tin of cookies.

Emma's eyes filled. "You came back."

"Couldn't resist the company," Clara smiled.

They spent the evening by the fire, the three of them sharing cocoa and stories. Clara laughed until tears formed in the corners of her eyes. She told them about sledding as a girl with her siblings, about the first Christmas she spent alone after her husband passed, and how she'd learned that joy could be quiet and still be real.

Lizzy listened, spellbound. "You make everything sound like it matters," she said.

Clara winked. "That's because it does, my dear."

When it grew late, the fire burned low. Clara rose, brushing crumbs from her skirt. "I should go before the roads freeze."

Emma frowned. "Stay. It's too cold."

But Clara only smiled. "Don't worry. I'm right where I'm supposed to be."

She hugged them both — long, warm, and sure — then stepped out into the snow. The flakes caught in her hair, like bits of light before the door closed softly behind her.

THE HOUSE FELL QUIET AGAIN, the clock ticking toward midnight. Emma and Lizzy sat in the afterglow of her presence, each feeling the same strange warmth, the same peace that words couldn't touch.

Then the phone rang.

Emma picked it up, half laughing. "She must have forgotten something already."

But the voice on the other end made her still.

"Emma?" a man said gently. "This is Mark, Clara's brother. I'm sorry — I just wanted you to know that we found a card with your address among her things, and ... Clara passed away three years ago this week."

The room seemed to tilt.

Emma's voice caught. "I'm sorry, what?"

"I know it's strange," he continued softly. "She talked about you often. Said you were the kind of friend who made her believe in Christmas again. I thought you should know."

Emma thanked him, her voice faint. When she hung up, the silence in the room was different — vast, holy.

Lizzy looked at her. "Mom? What is it?"

Emma's hands trembled as she whispered, "Clara ... she's gone. She's been gone for years."

Lizzy shook her head. "That's not possible. She was here."

"I know," Emma said, tears sliding down her cheeks. "I saw her. I touched her."

They turned slowly toward the window. Outside, fresh snow was falling — but in the middle of the front yard, a clear path curved through the drifts, ending at the gate. No footprints led away.

Lizzy whispered, "Do you think it was an angel?"

Emma nodded, voice trembling but full. "I think some friends never really leave."

The handmade star on the tree flickered then — a single, soft pulse of gold. The same light they'd seen the night before.

Neither spoke. They simply stood there, hand in hand, hearts open, certain of what they both knew but could never explain.

Reflection: Sometimes love visits in ways we can't understand — through a knock at the door, a voice we remember, a kindness that outlives the body it once wore.

Mother's Note: Where does the real magic lie for you in the season? Do you think miracles happen, but we ignore the signs? Can we ask for miracles?

_____

_____

_____

_____

Daughter's Note: Have you ever experienced something you can't explain? Do you think miracles can happen when we ask for them?

_____

_____

_____

_____

DAY 25 – CHRISTMAS MORNING

The morning light spilled softly through the frost-tipped windows, touching every corner of the house like a blessing. The fire had burned low, leaving only a gentle warmth that clung to the walls.

Lizzy stirred awake on the couch, still wrapped in the blanket from the night before. The tree glowed quietly in the corner — not bright, not showy, just steady. The handmade star shimmered faintly above it, the glow deep and golden, as if it were breathing.

For a long moment, Lizzy didn't move. She simply watched her mother.

Emma stood by the window, her robe pulled close, her face soft and thoughtful in the morning light. She wasn't rushing around like usual. There was no list, no plan — just stillness.

It was the first time Lizzy really saw her mother — not

just as "Mom," but as a woman who had lived and lost and kept loving anyway.

She thought about the letter. About the miracles they couldn't explain. About Clara. About the way her mother had tried, year after year, to keep Christmas glowing — even when the world went dim.

And for the first time, Lizzy understood.

All those moments she had rolled her eyes at — the baking, the ornaments, the lists, the stubborn cheer — they weren't chores. They were offerings. The way her mother said I love you to a world that sometimes forgot how to listen.

Emma turned then, and their eyes met. "You're awake," she said softly.

Lizzy nodded, her throat tight. "I didn't want to miss the morning."

Emma smiled gently. "You never do. You just don't always know you're part of it."

Lizzy and Emma sat down to open gifts with each other. They started with the gifts from Santa. Lizzy was delighted to see he remembered her curling iron and bedding. As she continued to unwrap another present, she stopped midway.

"Lizzy, her mom said, what's wrong honey, something not on your list?".

Lizzy whispered, "You've been doing this all these years — holding the light for both of us."

Emma reached out, brushing a stray hair from her

daughter's cheek. "It's what my mother did for me. I just didn't realize she was teaching me how to do it until I had you."

Lizzy felt tears spill down, warm and unhurried. "I think I get it now."

Emma smiled, her eyes glistening. "One day, you'll hold it too."

Her mom reached over and gave her a hug, grateful the days leading up to Christmas had been such a magical experience with her daughter.

"We need to open the last day", Emma said.

Lizzy opened the door, it read, "The greatest gift of Christmas is Love". Lizzy and Mom both looked at each other. "Well isn't that true", said Emma.

Lizzy crossed the room and sat beside her. For a moment, they both just looked at the tree. The light from the star seemed to dance across the walls — soft, pulsing, alive.

Lizzy looked back at the star — and in its glow, she thought she saw something move: the faint outline of two women standing together, hands intertwined, their faces gentle and proud.

She didn't blink. She didn't need to.

"Mom," she whispered, "do you see them?"

Emma's hand found hers, steady and warm. "Yes," she breathed. "I always do."

The vision faded as softly as snow melting into light.

But Lizzy didn't feel sad. She felt full — as if the miracle had moved inside her, finding a new home.

She looked at her mother again, and suddenly all the years ahead seemed brighter, softer, possible.

"Thank you," she whispered.

Emma smiled. "For what?"

Lizzy replied, "For keeping the light."

Emma kissed her forehead, knowing that the greatest gift of Christmas was sitting right in front of her. Santa really outdid himself this year, she thought to herself.

Outside, church bells began to ring in the distance — a melody carried by the wind, faint and pure. Emma and Lizzy would forever remember this Christmas as a miracle that would never be forgotten.

REFLECTION: Miracles come in many different forms, if we don't blink, we might just see the one that's been there all along.

Mother's Note: Do you ever see life through your daughter's eyes? What is the greatest gift you consider when you think about her? What do you treasure most about your daughter?

_____

_____

_____

_____

Daughter's Note: What is life like through your mother's eyes? What is the one thing you are most grateful for, that she has given you? What do you treasure most about your relationship?

_____

_____

_____

_____

ACKNOWLEDGMENTS

I would like to thank my dad for being an inspiration to me in in both life and literary; may we always follow our dreams. I would also like to thank Gary at Olive Publishing for support throughout the process as well as my family. I would like to thank Melissa in walking through this journey with me. Lastly, I would like to thank the mothers that go through the pains of parenthood but work every day to make life magical.

ABOUT THE AUTHOR

Laura Dover, LPCC is a Clinical Counselor and Motivational Coach with over twenty years of experience in the counseling field. Her passion lies in witnessing the transformative power of healing as she guides individuals through their theraputic journeys using diverse theraputic modalities tailored to each person's unique needs.

With two decades of dedicated practice, Laura has developed a deep understanding of the human capacity for growth and resilience. Her integrative approach combines evidence-based techniques with compassionate support, creating a safe place where healing can flourish.

When she's not supporting clients in their healing journeys, Laura cherishes time with her family who remain her greatest source of joy and inspiration.

BEFORE YOU GO

Before you go, I'd like to request a bit more of your time. If you found this book helpful, I would be so grateful if you would please leave a short review on Amazon.

Even if you read only one or two chapters, you could mention why those insights helped you on your journey or something you might avoid doing in the future. Books like this are often lost in a sea of books unless kind and generous readers like you take the time to post honest reviews. When reviews are posted, the algorithms take note and promote the book to other potential readers.

Thank you in advance for this generous expression of your appreciation. Your review will encourage me to spend more time sharing my advice with the public in this way. Being able to help others through writing means everything to me.

You can also email me directly with your thoughts at I'd love to hear from you here: laura.imely@gmail.com.

www.ingramcontent.com/pod-product-compliance
Lightning Source LLC
Chambersburg PA
CBHW071521120626
46550CB00006B/2302